CLASSIC MOUTH

**Monologues for Boys and Girls
from
Classic Literature**

Edited by Lydia Cosentino

Dramaline Publications

Dramaline Publications, 36-851 Palm View Rd., Rancho Mirage, CA 92270
Phone 619/770-6076 Fax 619/770-4507

Library of Congress Cataloging-in-Publication Data

Cosentino, Lydia.
    Classic Mouth:Monologues for Boys and Girls from
Classic Literature / edited by Lydia Cosentino
      p. cm.
    Summary: A collection of monologues adapted from such
    classic works of children's literature as "Alice in Wonderland,"
    "Little Women," "Pollyanna," Tom Sawyer, and "Great
    Expectations."
      ISBN 0-940669-35-8 (alk. paper)
      1. Acting—Juvenile literature. 2. Monologues—Juvenile
    literature. [1. Monologues.]
    PN2080.C5445 1996
    808.82' 45—dc20
                                    96-36422

Cover Design by John Sabel

This book is printed on 55# Glatfelter acid-free paper, a paper that meets the requirements of the American Standard of Permanence of paper for printed library material.

CONTENTS

Boys:

INTRODUCTION

Recognizing that young actors need good material of proper duration that provides them an opportunity to showcase their varied talents, I compiled these monologues mostly from classic literature (three are from other sources, but their classical style and provocative subject matter render them ideal for inclusion in this publication). Most of the material, however, is from classic children's literature and will appeal to boys and girls between the ages of six and fourteen. In most of the speeches, the speaker falls within this age range, though in a piece such as *Robinson Crusoe* (an adventure tale that is often included on a shelf of classic children's literature), he may be describing an event that occurred many years ago. The young actor performing Robinson Crusoe, therefore, may decide to focus on the young boy's rebellious nature rather than on the reflective character of the actual narrator. While Marianne from *Sense and Sensibility* is perhaps fifteen years old, she may be represented by a twelve- or thirteen-year-old actor. since it's her romantic nature that is revealed in her monologue. And Anne in *Anne of Green Gables* may be played older. The performers should be flexible with respect to age and use their imaginations regarding costumes and props and not be limited by the period in which the piece is set. If they concentrate on the dramatic situation of the monologue, they will find ample room for individual character interpretation.

The collection also includes pieces spoken by some of literature's most beloved animal characters, such as The

Ugly Duckling and Kenneth Graham's infamous Toad (of Toad Hall, of course) as well as his companions, Ratty and Mole. While these characters embody the spirit and charm of both boys and girls, I have placed them in the boys' section. However, each of the speeches I selected (such as Rat's rhapsody on river life or Mole's hysterical outburst about his lost home) provides an effective dramatic showcase for any actor.

Since these works are in the public domain, I freely adapted the speeches as monologues. In some instances, for example, I created a monologue by deleting the dialogue of other characters; in other scenes, I merged a series of comments into a monologue; in others, I added details to give the monologue dramatic shape. For each piece I provided a plot summary and set the scene as well as described the character, so that even if the actors have not read the story (or seen the movie), they will be informed about context. Where necessary (that is, where the speech itself doesn't make it clear), I also offer suggestions about costume, dramatic movement, and character traits that will aid the actors in developing a well-rounded character.

These suggestions, of course, are offered to engage— not limit—young actors' imaginations. Actors should also remember that they are not confined to the original period in terms of costume or props. If they choose to present the character in a modern setting or costume, they should do so.

These monologues may also be used in an acting class to help young actors develop a variety of voices and character types by recreating the voices of heroes and heroines from classic literature. The dramatic monologue encourages the actors' skill in creating a scene through the presentation of character, and with the aid of background notes and suggestions, young actors can practice the dramatic rendition of character. In order to dramatically recreate the scene, actors may wish to learn something about the period in which the action occurs. Such background knowledge equips young actors to achieve the variety today's filmmaking seems to require, with its focus so often on these classic periods. For example, *Robinson Crusoe* and *Sense and Sensibility*, two popular films, are represented here. In addition to this, actors may wish to read the original story in order to fully conceptualize the monologue and gain insight into the character's many facets.

Besides inspiring young actors, these monologues may contribute voices to library and bookstore reading programs that are fast becoming Saturday and summer staples. What better way to bring literature to life than with the voices of the characters who inhabit its pages? With minimal attention to costume and props, readers may *become* a character or characters, thereby ensuring, through dramatic presentation, not only the interest of their young auditors, but perhaps their actual involvement.

The classroom itself may provide another home for these voices. Besides giving teachers a chance to reintroduce role-playing and recitation as a means of enlivening literature, these monologues may instill an interest in students to read the original story. In addition to provoking a literary interest, these monologues can be taught as social documents, providing a starting point for historical and sociological research and discussion. After all, characters are themselves products of historical, sociological, and political circumstances, and the literature that showcases them is itself a product of these same forces. Depending on the level of the class and the teacher's interests, these voices may help bring life to material that might otherwise remain dormant.

Whether as audition pieces, practice pieces, readings, or study aids, these timeless voices continue to bring pleasure to all who hear them. Rediscovering them has given me great pleasure indeed, and, hopefully, young presenters will experience this same pleasure as they bring to life some of the great characters in classical literature.

GIRLS' MONOLOGUES

AESOP'S FABLES

The country maid is a character from an Aesop fable by that name, so, like all fables, it has a moral—that is, a lesson to teach. In this speech, the maid is not paying attention to what she's doing because she's fantasizing about the future—that is, "counting her chickens before they're hatched" or anticipating a future good but neglecting a present task. She should be swinging the pail absent-mindedly while speaking.

The presenter, dressed in rustic clothes that are clean but patched, might twirl around and spread out her skirt, always endangering the contents of the pail until, finally, either with a toss of her head or a gesture, she spills its contents. Her tone is dreamy and, as she continues, she grows more and more excited until she spills the milk. At the end, she speaks sadly and wistfully.

COUNTRY MAID

I shall sell this milk when I get to the village, and with the money I get for it I shall buy 300 eggs. Of course, some of the eggs may be bad, so only 250 of them will hatch into little chicks. The chicks will be grown by Christmas time and then I will take them into the market and sell them. Poultry always gets a high price at Christmas time, so I shall make a lot of money. With the money I shall buy me a new gown. I think it will be green. Or perhaps it should be blue. No, I am prettier in green. I shall buy a new green gown and I shall wear it to the fair on May Day. Naturally, all the young fellows will want to dance with me, but not one of them shall be my partner. I should refuse them all.

(*Tossing her head proudly, or, if she carries the pail, flinging out her hand in a gesture of dismissal, upsetting the milk pail*) All the milk spilled on the ground! Now there will be no money, no eggs, no chickens, and no green dress!

Perhaps I *should not* have counted my chickens before they were hatched.

ALICE in WONDERLAND

Alice, from Lewis Carroll's Alice in Wonderland, *is sitting in a field with her sister, who is reading a book with no pictures or conversation in it,. She is bored until she sees a white rabbit hurry by, taking a watch out of his vest pocket, and say, "Oh dear! Oh dear! I shall be too late!" Burning with curiosity, she jumps up and follows it just in time to see it pop down a large rabbit hole under a hedge. Without thinking, Alice jumps down after him, never once considering how in the world she will get out again. The rabbit hole goes straight like a tunnel for some distance, and Alice finds herself falling down what seems to be a deep well. She falls very slowly and has plenty of time to look about her—and to wonder what is going to happen next. She sees cupboards and bookshelves and maps and pictures just like living rooms and kitchens as she falls past.*

The speaker may try to give an impression of falling, perhaps rolling a few times in between speaking. Alice is usually represented as a proper Victorian child somewhere between the age of seven and ten years old. Her hair is held back by a ribbon and her dress is covered by a smock or apron. Her tone is light and whimsical; she is without fear. Since she falls so slowly, she begins to think aloud to pass the time. Alice speaks the following to herself as she falls:

ALICE

After such a fall as this, I shall think nothing about tumbling downstairs! How brave they'll all think me at home! Why, I wouldn't say anything about it, even if I fell off the top of the house! (*Pausing, continuing to fall*) I wonder how many miles I've fallen by this time? I must be getting somewhere near the center of the earth. Let me see: that would be 4000 miles down, I think—yes, that's about the right distance—but then I wonder what latitude or longitude I've got to? (*Pausing, falling*) I wonder if I shall fall right *through* the earth! How funny it'll seem to come out among the people that walk with their heads downwards! The antipathies, I think—but I shall have to ask them what the name of the country is, you know. Please, Ma'am, is this New Zealand? Or Australia? (*She tries to curtsey as she speaks*) And what an ignorant little girl she'll think me for asking! No, it'll never do to ask: perhaps I shall see it written up somewhere. (*Musing*) My cat Dinah'll miss me very much tonight, I should think! I hope they'll remember her saucer of milk at teatime. Dinah, my dear! I wish you were down here with me! There are no mice in the air, I'm afraid, but you might catch a bat, and that's very like a mouse, you know. But do cats eat bats, I wonder? (*Growing sleepy, mumbling to herself*) Do bats eat *cats*? Do cats eat bats? (*Almost asleep, dreamily*) Do *cats* eat *bats*? Now, Dinah, tell me the truth: did you ever eat a bat? (*Waking up with a thump as she hits bottom and stops falling*) Oh!

A MAID

The maid of all work is "A neat, bright, clever, stumpy little thing, with a sweet sort of merry voice," said Anne Thackeray (1873–1919), who recorded the maid's account.

This description suggests that the mistreatment of some heroines of stories and fairy tales, like Cinderella or Sleeping Beauty, are closer to fact than a twentieth-century reader might expect. Child labor was common in Europe in the seventeeth, eighteenth, and nineteenth centuries.

A MAID

Oh, I've been a servant for years! I learnt ironing off the lady; I didn't know nothing about it. I didn't know nothing about anything. I didn't know where to buy the wood for the fire. (*Exploding with laughter*) I run along the street and asked the first person I saw where the wood-shop was. I was frightened—oh, I was. They wasn't particular kind in my first place. I had plenty to eat—it wasn't anything of that. They jest give me an egg, and they says, "There, get your dinner," but not any more. I had to do all the work. I'd no one to go to: Oh! I cried the first night. I used to cry so. (*Laughing*) I had always sleep in a ward full of other girls, and there I was all alone, and this was a great big house—oh, so big! and they told me to go downstairs, in a room by the kitchen all alone, with a long black passage. I might have screamed, but nobody woulda heard. An architect the gentleman was. I got to break everything . . . oh, I was frightened!

PEPPER and SALT

Christine is the youngest sister in the fairy tale "The Apple of Contentment" *from* Pepper and Salt *by Howard Pyle. Because she is not pretty, her two sisters (who dress in their Sunday clothes every day and sit in the sun doing nothing) make her take the geese out every day and feed her only on their leftovers. She should look very poor and hungry, but by the time she recounts her adventure and shows her seed, she is dancing with joy.*

CHRISTINE

One morning I started off to the hills along the dusty road, the geese straggling ahead, until, by and by, I came to a place where a bridge crossed the brook, and what should I see there but a little red cap, with a silver bell at the point of it, hanging from the alder branch. It was such a nice, pretty, little, red cap that I thought I would take it home with me, for I had never seen the like of it before. So I put it in my pocket and off I went with my geese again. I had hardly gone a step when I heard a voice calling me, "Christine! Christine!"

I looked, and what should I see but a queer, little, gray man, with a head as big as a cabbage, and little legs as thin as young radishes. "What do you want?" I asked when the little man had come to where I was.

Oh, the little man wanted his cap, for without it he could not go back home into the hill—that was where he belonged. He would give me five dollars for it and gladly; no, I did not care for money. What else would he give for this nice, dear, little cap?

"I will give you this for the cap," he replied, showing me something in his hand that looked just like a bean, but as black as a lump of coal. "That is a seed from the apple of contentment. Plant it, and from it will grow a tree, and from the tree an apple. Everybody in the world that sees the apple will long for it, but nobody in the world can pluck it but you. It will always be meat and drink to you when you are hungry, and warm clothes to you when you are cold. Moreover, as soon as you pluck it from the tree, another will grow in its place. Now, will you give me my hat?"

"Oh yes, I would give the little man his hat for such a seed as that, and gladly! " So he gave me the seed, and I gave him his cap. He put it on and—puff!—away he was gone, as suddenly as the light of a candle when you blow it out! But I hardly looked at him—I was *so* happy to have the magic seed!

STREET PEOPLE of LONDON

The watercress girl (like the maid on page 7) is a working child about eight years old in ninth-entury England (her account is recorded in a nineteenth century report for Parliament that was trying to legislate child labor). She is probably not very clean, and her clothing should be ragged. She seems older because she reports her experience in such a matter-of-fact way, seemingly unaware of how terrible her account is. She has little education, so this should be apparent in her accent and speech.

THE WATERCRESS GIRL

I go about the streets with watercresses crying, "Four bunches a penny, watercresses." I am just eight years old—that's all, and I've got a big sister, and a brother and a sister younger than me. On and off, I've been in the streets about a year. Before that, I had to take care of a baby for my aunt. It wasn't heavy—it was only two months old; but I minded it for such a long time—till it could walk. It was a very nice little baby, not a very pretty one; but, if I touched it under the chin, it would laugh. Before I had the baby, I used to help mother, who was in the fur trade; and, if there was any slits in the fur, I'd sew them up. My mother learned me how to needle-work and to knit when I was about five. I used to go to school, too; but I wasn't there long. I've forgot about it now, it's such a time ago; and mother took me away be-cause the master whacked me, though the missus never used to touch me. I didn't like him at all. What do you think? He hit me three times, really hard, across the face with his cane, and made me go dancing downstairs; and when mother saw the marks on my cheek, she went to blow him up, but she couldn't see him—he was afraid. Anyway, that's why I left school.

ANNE of GREEN GABLES

Anne Shirley is a very romantic girl who is about eleven years old. In the story Anne of Green Gables *by Lucy Maud Montgomery, Anne is an orphan brought to live on a farm with a childless couple (Matthew Cuthbert, a taciturn bachelor farmer, and his reserved spinster sister, Marilla), where Anne's enthusiasm and dramatic intensity often clash with Marilla's down-to-earth values. In a magazine of the period, Anne is described as "droll one minute, pathetic the next; staid and wise as a grandmother one minute, bubbling over with impish mischief the next," yet always "lovable." Mark Twain, creator of Tom Sawyer and Huck Finn, described Anne as "the most moving and delightful" and "dearest" heroine "since the immortal Alice." In this scene, Anne is working on a patchwork quilt (a practical activity), but patchwork is a particularly unsatisfying kind of sewing, Anne says; it doesn't satisfy her imaginative nature. This speech reveals Anne's bubbly nature and her ability to talk, almost without taking a breath. She's probably wearing a simple dress and braids and sewing a piece of patchwork.*

ANNE

I do *not* like patchwork. I think some kinds of sewing would be nice; but there's no scope for imagination in patchwork. It's just one little seam after another and you never seem to be getting anywhere. But, of course, I'd rather be Anne of Green Gables sewing patchwork than Anne of any other place with nothing to do but play. I wish time went as quick sewing patches as it does when

I'm playing with Diana, though. Oh, we do have such elegant times. I have to furnish most of the imagination, but I'm well able to do that. Diana is simply perfect in every other way. You know that little piece of land across the brook that runs up between our farm and Mr. Barry's? It belongs to Mr. William Bell, and right in the corner there is a little ring of white birch trees—the most romantic spot. Diana and I have our playhouse there. We call it Idlewild. Isn't that a poetical name? I assure you it took me some time to think it out. I stayed awake nearly a whole night before I invented it. Then, just as I was dropping off to sleep, it came like an inspiration. Diana was *enraptured* when she heard it. We have got our house fixed up elegantly. You must come and see it—won't you?

This speech gives more scope to Anne's romantic imagination. The words tumble out breathlessly, and Anne moves about constantly as she speaks, using many gestures.

ANNE
Second Speech

Oh, we have named that little round pool over there in Mr. Barry's field Willowmere. I got that name out of the book Diana lent me. That was a thrilling book. The heroine had five lovers. I'd be satisfied with one, wouldn't you? She was very handsome and she went through great tribulations. She could faint as easy as anything. I'd love to be able to faint, wouldn't you? It's so romantic. But I'm really very healthy for as thin as I am. I believe I'm getting fatter, though. Don't you think I am? I look at my elbows every morning when I get up to see if any dimples are coming. Diana is having a new dress made with elbow sleeves. She is going to wear it to the picnic. Oh, I do hope it will be fine next Wednesday. I don't feel that I could endure the disappointment if anything happened to prevent me from getting to the picnic. I suppose I'd live through it, but I'm certain it would be a lifelong sorrow. It wouldn't matter if I got to a hundred picnics in after years; they wouldn't make up for missing this one. They're going to have boats on the Lake of Shining Waters—and ice cream, as I told you. I have never tasted ice cream. Diana tried to explain what it was like, but I guess ice cream is one of those things that is beyond imagination.

Anne of Anne of Green Gables *is rhapsodic in this speech as she recounts her wonderful afternoon with her friend Diana. Anne had been forbidden to play with Diana, her very best friend, because Diana's mother thought Anne had gotten Diana tipsy. Anne was in despair, but she has just returned from Diana's house, where Diana's mother forgave Anne and lifted the ban against their friendship. You may want to stop after the poetry verse.*

ANNE
Third Speech

You see before you a perfectly happy person. I'm perfectly happy—yes, in spite of my red hair. Mrs. Barry kissed me and cried and said she was so sorry and she could never repay me. I felt fearfully embarrassed, but I just said as politely as I could, "I have no hard feelings for you, Mrs. Barry. I assure you once and for all that I did not mean to intoxicate Diana and that henceforth I shall cover the past with the mantle of oblivion." That was a pretty dignified way of speaking, wasn't it? I felt that I was heaping coals of fire on Mrs. Barry's head. And Diana and I had a lovely afternoon. Diana showed me a new, fancy crochet stitch her aunt over at Carmody taught her. Not a soul in Avonlea knows it but us, and we pledged a solemn vow never to reveal it to anyone else. Diana gave me a beautiful card with a wreath of roses on it and a verse of poetry:

> *If you love me as I love you*
> *Nothing but death can part us two.*

And that is true. We're going to ask Mr. Phillips to let us sit together in school again, and Gertie Pye can go with Minnie Andrews. We had an elegant tea. Mrs. Barry had the very best china set out, just as if I was real company. I can't tell you what a thrill it gave me. Nobody ever used their very best china on my account before. And we had fruitcake and poundcake and doughnuts and two kinds of preserves. And Mrs. Barry asked me if I took tea and said, "Pa, why don't you pass the biscuits to Anne?" It must be lovely to be grown up, when just being treated as if you were so nice . . . Well, anyway, when I am grown up, I'm always going to talk to little girls as if they were, too, and I'll never laugh when they use big words. I know from sorrowful experience how that hurts one's feelings.

WOMAN'S WORK

Peggy in Woman's Work *works in a coal mine, as she describes. She works hard and is treated poorly. She should look abused and be dressed badly. The dirt should look ingrained like coal dust, and she should have a timid air, perhaps ducking her head when she speaks, as if she's used to being abused. Her account is recorded in nineteenth-century Parliamentarian records investigating child labor.*

PEGGY

They call me Peggy for my nickname down here, but my right name is Margaret; I am about nine years, or going on nine; I have been at work in the pit thrusting baskets above a year; come in the morning sometimes at seven o'clock, sometimes half-past seven, and I go sometimes home at six o'clock, sometimes at seven when I do overtime. I get my breakfast of porridge before I come, and bring a piece of muffin, which I eat on coming to pit; I get my lunch at twelve o'clock, which is a dry muffin, and sometimes butter on it, but have no time allowed to stop and eat it. I eat it while I am thrusting the load; I get no break, but get some supper when I get home, and then go to bed when I have washed me; and am very tired . . . They flog us down in the pit, sometimes with their hand upon my bottom, which hurts me very much; Thomas Copeland flogs me more than once in a day, which makes me cry. There are two other girls working with me, and there was four, but one left because she had the belly-ache; I am poorly myself sometimes with bellyache, and sometimes headache. I had rather play than go into the pit; I get fifty cents a day, but I had rather set cards for fifty cents a day than go into the pit. The men often swear at me; many times they say, "Damn thee," and other times (*Whispers*) "Goddamn thee, and such like, Peggy."

REBECCA of SUNNYBROOK FARM

Rebecca of Sunnybrook Farm by Kate Douglas Wiggin tells the story of ten-year-old Rebecca, who is sent to live with her spinster aunts, Miranda and Jane, because the family farm is too poor to support all of the children. Rebecca is used to a large, chaotic, crowded family life very unlike the quiet Riverboro residence of her aunts. Her zest for life often proves too lively for her quiet aunts, and her irrepressible nature seems undisciplined, especially to the strict Miranda. In this scene, Rebecca is conjugating verb tenses for her teacher. Rebecca's imaginative nature is revealed in this scene. She might use a slate or have the verb tenses written on a board during this speech. Rebecca is very dramatic in her presentation and speaks earnestly.

REBECCA

I might have been glad.
You might have been glad.
He, she, it might have been glad.

(*Thoughtfully*) Miss Dearborn says "he" or "she" might have been glad but "it" couldn't have been glad because "it" is neuter gender, but I asked if we couldn't say, "The kitten might have been glad if it had known it was not going to be drowned." Miss Dearborn said a kitten was actually masculine or feminine gender.

Then I asked, "Is a hollyhock neuter?" (*Pause, pondering*) Couldn't we say, "The hollyhock might have been glad to see the rain, but there was a weak little hollyhock bud growing out of its stalk, and it was afraid that that might be hurt by the storm; so the big hollyhock was kind of afraid, instead of being real glad"? (*Considering*) I think they are, anyway. Now what shall I say? (*Concentrating*)

> If thou hadst known.
> If he had known.
> If we had known.
> If you had known.
> If they had known.

(*Dismayed*) Oh, it is the saddest tense! Nothing but *ifs, ifs, ifs!* And it makes you feel that if they only *had* known, things might have been better!

Another character from Rebecca of Sunnybrook Farm *is Huldah, one of the rich girls in Riverboro. Huldah is vain and overbearing; she probably has ringlets and wears a pink and ruffly dress. She pirouettes and shows off her feet and French boots as she speaks.*

HULDAH

May I dry my feet at your register? I can't bear to wear rubbers unless the mud or the slush is simply knee-deep; they make your feet look so awfully big. I had such a fuss getting this pair of French-heeled boots that I don't intend to spoil the looks of them with rubbers any oftener than I can help. I believe boys notice feet quicker than anything. Elmer Webster stepped on one of mine yesterday, when I accidentally had it out in the aisle, and when he apologized after class, he said he wasn't so much to blame, for the foot was so little he really couldn't see it! Isn't he perfectly great? Of course, that's only his way of talking, for, after all, I only wear a number two; but these French heels and pointed toes do certainly make your foot look smaller, and it's always said a high instep helps, too. I used to think mine was almost a deformity, but they say it's a great beauty. Just put your feet beside mine, girls, and look at the difference; not that I care much, but just for fun.

POLLYANNA

Pollyanna (from Eleanor H. Porter's novel of that name), an
orphan, has come to live with her Aunt Polly, a spinster, after
Pollyanna's minister father has died. Aunt Polly, however, has
never met Pollyanna because she disapproved of her sister's
marriage. Pollyanna is trying to be brave and to follow her father's advice to find something to be glad about in any situation. She's attempting to be optimistic despite her grief and despite her fear at meeting a previously unknown and unwelcom-
ing relative. She fights back tears in this speech, determined to
be cheerful. She may cry or come close to crying when she
speaks of her father's going to heaven, but she determinedly
brightens up in the last line. If you want to shorten the speech,
you might begin with the second paragraph or use only that
section from "I ought to have explained . . ." and stop at " . . .
but not the black part."

POLLYANNA

Isn't this lovely? Is it far? I hope so—I love to ride! Of
course, if it isn't far, I don't mind either 'cause I'll be glad
to get there all the sooner, you know. What a pretty
street! I knew it was going to be pretty; Father told me . . .
(*She stops with a little choking breath. Then she hurries on
with a brave lifting of her head*) I ought to have explained
before. Mrs. Gray told me to, at once—about this red
gingham dress, you know, and why I'm not in black. She
said you'd think 'twas queer. But there weren't any black
things in the last missionary barrel, only a lady's velvet
petticoat that Deacon Carr's wife said wasn't suitable for

me at all. Besides, it had white spots—worn, you know—on both elbows, and some other places. Part of the Ladies' Aid wanted to buy me a black dress and hat, but the other part thought the money ought to go toward the red carpet they're trying to get—for the church, you know. Mrs. White said maybe it was just as well, anyway, for she didn't like children in black—that is, I mean, she liked the children, of course, but not the black part. (*Thoughtful*) Of course, 'twould have been a good deal harder to be glad in black—(*Rushing to explain*)—that father's gone to heaven to be with mother and the rest of us, you know. He said I must be glad. But it's been pretty hard to—to do it, even in red gingham, because I— I wanted him so. And I couldn't help feeling I *ought* to have him, 'specially as mother and the rest have God and all the angels, while I didn't have anybody but the Ladies' Aid. (*Brightening*) But now I'm sure it'll be easier because I've got you, Aunt Polly. I'm so glad I've got you!

LORNA DOONE

Lorna Doone is "the little maid whose beauty and whose kindness made me yearn to be with her," and whose hair is a "black shower" that falls to the ground among the first primroses of the season so that "I think of her, through all the rough storms of my life, when I see an early primrose," says John Ridd, who rescues Lorna in R. D. Blackmore's romantic adventure tale of feuding Scottish families, Lorna Doone.

Lorna is about thirteen years old. Her beauty and kindliness seem at odds with her rough relatives.

LORNA DOONE

I have no remembrance now of father, or of mother; although they say that my father was the eldest son of Sir Ensor Doone, and the bravest, and the best of them. And so they call me heiress to this little realm of violence; and in sorry sport sometimes, I am their princess, or their queen.

Many people living here, as I am forced to do, would perhaps be very happy, and perhaps I ought to be so. We have a beauteous valley, the grass is so fresh, and the brook so bright and lively, and flowers of so many hues come after one another, that no one need be dull, if only left alone with them.

But all around me is violence and robbery, coarse delight and savage pain, reckless joke and hopeless death. Is it any wonder that I cannot sink with these, that I cannot so forget my soul, as to live the life of brutes, and die the death more horrible because it dreams of waking?

There is none to lead me forward, there is none to teach me right; young as I am, I live beneath a curse that lasts forever.

UNCLE TOM'S CABIN

Harriet Beecher Stowe's novel Uncle Tom's Cabin *is a nineteenth-century indictment of slavery that earned its author Abraham Lincoln's legendary comment, "So this is the little lady who made this big war." The author says, "The object of these sketches is to awaken sympathy and feeling for the African race, as they exist among us." There are many unforgettable characters in this much-read and frequently performed work. There's Uncle Tom, the slave, and Simon Legree, the cruel slave-driver whose name has become synonymous with cruelty. The two children are best remembered, however— Little Eva and Topsy. Little Eva is the dying daughter of the plantation owner who shows true Christian compassion in the midst of evil; Topsy is the little slave girl who is the same age as Eva, but unlike Eva has known nothing of love or mercy. In this scene, Eva has called the slaves to her deathbed to say goodby. She is the picture of goodness and kindness, but she is weak and dying.*

LITTLE EVA

I sent for you all, my dear friends, because I love you. I love you all; and I have something to say to you, which I want you always to remember . . . I am going to leave you. In a few more weeks you will see me no more—

(*Quieting her distraught audience*) If you love me, you must not interrupt me. Listen to what I say. I want to speak to you about your souls . . . Many of you, I am afraid, are very careless. You are thinking only about this world. I want you to remember that there is a beautiful world where Jesus is. I am going there, and you can go there. It is for you as much as me. But, if you want to go there, you must not live idle, careless, thoughtless lives. You must be Christians. You must remember that each one of you can become angels, and be angels forever . . . if you want to be Christians, Jesus will help you. You must pray to him; you must read—(*She breaks off, realizing they can't read*)

(*Shaking her head*) I have prayed for you; and I know Jesus will help you even if you can't read the Bible. Try all to do the best you can; pray every day; ask him to help you, and get the Bible read to you whenever you can; and I think I shall see you all in heaven.

There isn't one of you that hasn't always been very kind to me; and I want to give you something that, when you look at, you shall always remember me. I'm going to give all of you a curl of my hair; and, when you look at it, think that I loved you and am gone to heaven, and that I want to see you all there.

Topsy speaks here. She's angry and rebellious, and despite her words, we sense she'd like to be loved. Her pain must be made apparent beneath her belligerent words.

TOPSY

Spects it's my wicked heart makes me behave so bad. Miss Feely, she done all she could fo' me—Ol' Missus always say so, too. Lor', yes, she whipped me a heap harder, and used to pull my har, and knock my head agin the door; but it didn't do me no good! I spects, if they's to pull every spear o' har out o' my head, it wouldn't do no good, neither—I's so wicked!

Dunno nothin' bout love—I loves candy and sich, that's all. Never had no fambly; ain't never had nothin' nor nobody.

Even Miss Feely, she can't bar me, 'cause I's colored—she'd's soon have a toad touch her! There can't nobody love coloreds, and coloreds can't do nothin'. I don't care—

(*Philosophical*) Couldn't never be nothin' but colored, if I was ever so good. If I could be skinned, and come white, I might try then.

LITTLE WOMEN

Louisa May Alcott's Little Women *has delighted readers since its publication. The Marches' cheerfulness and love despite their poverty continues to appeal to modern audiences, as evidenced by its recent film popularity.*

The four daughters—Meg (the oldest), Jo (the writer and tomboy), Beth (the sweet one), and Amy (the youngest)—and their mother struggle through hard times during the American Civil War. Amy is the vainest of the sisters and, as the youngest, is perhaps a bit spoiled. She's artistic, but cannot deny a certain attraction to pretty things and to a wealthier lifestyle than the Marches can afford.

AMY

I think being disgraced in school is a great deal *tryinger* *
than anything bad boys can do. Susie Perkins came to
school today with a lovely, red, carnelian** ring; I wanted
it dreadfully, and wished I was her with all my might.
Well, she drew a picture of Mr. Davis, with a monstrous
nose and a hump, and the words, "Young ladies, my eye
is upon you!" coming out of his mouth in a balloon thing.
We were laughing over it, when all of a sudden his eye
was on us, and he ordered Susie to bring up her slate. She
was *parry*lized with fright, but she went, and oh, what *do*
you think he did? He took her by the ear—the ear! Just
fancy how horrid!—and led her to the recitation

---

* *more trying*

** *precious, red gem*

platform, and made her stand there half an hour, holding that slate so everyone could see.

We sat as still as mice; and Susie cried quarts, I know she did. I didn't envy her then; for I felt that millions of carnelian rings wouldn't have made me happy, after that. I never, never should have got over such an agonizing mortification.

Beth is the gentle sister who contracts the Hummel baby's fever. Her compassion and kindness are apparent in this speech.

BETH

Mrs. Hummel's baby's dead! It died in my lap before she got home. It was so sad. I saw in a minute that it was sicker, but Lottchen said her mother had gone for a doctor, so I took baby and let Lotty rest. It seemed asleep, but all of a sudden it gave a little cry, and trembled, and then lay very still. I tried to warm its feet, and Lotty gave it some milk, but it didn't stir, and I knew it was dead.

I sat and held it softly till Mrs. Hummel came with the doctor. He said it was dead, and looked at Heinrich and Minna, who have got sore throats. "Scarlet fever, Ma'am. Ought to have called me before," he said crossly. Mrs. Hummel told him she was poor, and had tried to cure baby herself, but now it was too late, and she could only ask him to help the others, and trust to charity for his pay. He smiled then, and was kinder; but it was very sad, and I cried with them till he turned around, all of a sudden, and told me to go home and take belladonna right away, or I'd have the fever. I didn't want to leave, but Mrs. Hummel made me. Oh! I felt so bad for Mrs. Hummel and baby!

Jo is the rebellious daughter, the writer, the one who has the most difficult time becoming "a lady." Beth is her favorite sister; she's gentle and kind and often helps and comforts Jo. When Beth becomes ill with scarlet fever, it is Jo who suffers most.

Here she has just come from Beth's bedside, and the doctor has suggested the girls send for their mother, who is away attending their war-wounded father. Jo fears Beth may die.

JO

I've sent for mother. (*Wringing her hands*) The doctor told us to. (*Pacing to and fro agitatedly*) That must mean Beth's worse—maybe she'll die! Oh no! I won't think that! It couldn't happen! But she doesn't know us; she doesn't even talk about the flocks of green doves, as she calls the vine-leaves on the wall; she doesn't look like my Beth, and there's nobody to help us bear it; mother and father both gone, and God seems so far away I can't find Him! (*Tears pour down her cheeks. She stretches her hand in a helpless sort of way, as if groping in the dark. After sobbing a minute, pulling herself together with visible force*) I'm better now; I don't feel so forlorn and will try to bear it if it comes. (*Starts pacing again*) I'll keep hoping for the best—that's the way. Soon mother will be here, and then everything will be all right. At least father is better, so she won't feel so bad leaving him. Oh, me! It does seem as if all the troubles came in a heap, and I got the heaviest part on my shoulders (*Spreading her wet handkerchief across her knees*) I know Meg tries to pull fair, but she can't love Bethy as I do; and she won't miss her as I shall. Beth is my conscience, and I *can't* give her up. I can't! I can't! (*She cries despairingly, then looks up hopefully*) She's so good, and we all love her so much, I don't believe God will take her away yet. (*Once again crying, groans*) The good and dear people always do die, though! (*Catching herself again*) There, there! I've got to stop! Mother will be here soon; she musn't find me so upset! I'll just go back to Beth—that's what I'll do! I won't believe she'll die. I won't!

SENSE and SENSIBILITY

Jane Austen's novel Sense and Sensibility *still makes modern audiences laugh and cry. The two sisters, Elinor and Marianne, represent sensible love versus grand passion. Elinor is cool in judgment, possesses a strength of understanding, and has strong feelings that she knows how to manage. Marianne, however, knows no moderation with regard to her emotions. She is also generous, amiable, and interesting, but because she lacks control, she flings herself headlong into an inappropriate love with the undeserving Willoughby. After she believes they have fallen in love, she finds out that Willoughby is engaged to someone else. At a party in London, he has pretended not to remember their engagement, and Marianne, in her direct fashion, demands an explanation, still unwilling to accept that she has been deceived.*

MARIANNE

What am I to imagine by your behavior last night? I demand an explanation of it. I have passed a wretched night in endeavoring to excuse a conduct which can scarcely be called less than insulting; but though I have not yet been able to form any reasonable apology for your behavior, I am perfectly ready to hear your justification of it.

You have perhaps been misinformed, or purposely deceived, in something concerning me which may have lowered me in your opinion. Tell me what it is, explain the grounds on which you acted, and I shall be satisfied in being able to satisfy *you*. It would grieve me indeed to be obliged to think ill of you, but if I am to do it, if I am to learn that you are not what we have hitherto believed you, that your regard for us all was insincere, that your behavior to me was intended only to deceive, let it be told as soon as possible.

My feelings are at present in a state of dreadful indecision; I wish to acquit you, but certainty on either side will be ease to what I now suffer. If your sentiments are no longer what they were, you will return my notes, and the lock of my hair which is in your possession.

THE MILL on the FLOSS

Maggie Tulliver in George Eliot's The Mill on the Floss *is the rebellious heroine who rejects female limitations. She's smarter than her brother, but that is not considered a good female quality. Her father says, "She understands what one's talking about so as never was. And you should hear her read—straight off, as if she know'd it all beforehand. And allays at her book! But it's bad—it's bad; a woman's no business wi' being so clever; it'll turn to trouble."*

In this scene, Maggie, about eight years old, is looking at a book, The History of the Devil *by Daniel Defoe, and saying what the pictures mean.*

MAGGIE

It's a dreadful picture, isn't it? But I can't help looking at it. That old woman in the water's a witch—they've put her in to find out whether she's a witch or no, and if she swims she's a witch, and if she's drowned—and killed, you know—she's innocent, and not a witch, but only a poor, silly, old woman.

(*Perplexed*) But what good would it do her then, you know, when she was drowned? Only I suppose she'd go to heaven, and God would make it up to her. And this dreadful blacksmith with his arms akimbo, laughing—oh, isn't he ugly?—I'll tell you what he is.

He's the devil *really*—(*Agitated, growing louder*)—and not a right blacksmith; for the devil takes the shape of wicked men, and walks about and sets people doing wicked things, and he's oftener in the shape of a bad man than any other, because, you know, if people saw he was the devil, and he roared at 'em, they'd run away, and he couldn't make 'em do what he pleased!

JANE EYRE

In Jane Eyre *by Charlotte Brontë an orphan (Jane) is first left
with her Aunt Reed, then sent to Lowood (a school for poor
girls), and finally sent as a governess to Thornfield. Besides
being friendless, Jane is also plain, an unusual state for heroines. In this passage, Jane (about eight or nine years old) has
been locked in an upstairs room for biting her cousin John (who
hit her) and having, according to her Aunt, a temper tantrum.
Jane's sense of aggrieved injustice adds fuel to her anger, but
the coldness of the room and her fear in the growing darkness
overcome her anger.*

JANE

Unjust! Unjust! (*Stamping her foot and sobbing*) Why do I
thus suffer? I am nobody here! I have nothing in har-
mony with Mrs. Reed or her children! They do not love
me! I do not love them! I am not like them; I am useless,
incapable of serving their interest or adding to their pleasure. If I were happy, careless, romping, handsome, they
would tolerate me better. I am plain and passionate and
proud, so they hate me. They lock me up here in the red
room alone. (*Looking around apprehensively*) I grow cold as
stone. My anger dies down like embers on a dying fire.
(*Earnestly*) It must be most irksome for her to find herself
bound by a hard-wrung pledge to stand in the stead of a
parent to a strange child—whom she cannot love.
    (*Her fear increases and she looks around uneasily*) Oh!
what was that sound? Was it wings? Oh! I am afraid here
in the growing dark! (*Screaming*) Take me out! Let me go

into the nursery! Oh! I saw a light, and I thought a ghost had come! Oh, aunt, have pity! Forgive me! I cannot endure it—let me be punished some other way! I shall be killed if—Oh! Don't lock the door! (*She collapses in sobs*)

HEIDI

In Heidi by Johanna Spyri, the young and orphaned heroine is brought by her aunt to a Swiss mountain village to live with her grandfather. While on the mountain, Heidi becomes friends with the goat-boy, Peter. Neither Heidi nor Peter like school; they prefer to play with the goats in the mountain meadow. Therefore ,she and Peter are almost as untamed and uneducated as the goats. Heidi, however, has learned to read from Klara's (her friend's) kind grandmother, who told her that she could learn to read if she believed she could.

Here ,Heidi offers to teach the disinterested Peter how to read, threatening him with the dire consequences of refusing to do so.

HEIDI

I will teach you to read. I know quite well how. You must learn, and then read a hymn or two to the grandmother every day. (*Sensing resistance, threatening*) Or I can tell you what will happen if you do not learn. Your mother has already said that you must go to Frankfurt to learn all sorts of things, and I know where the boys go to school there. (*Menacing*) But in Frankfurt they do not stop going to school when they grow up, but keep on even after they are big men. I saw that myself. And you need not think there is only one teacher there as we have here, and such a good one, too. No, whole rows of masters go together into the schoolhouse, and they are all in black as if they were going to church, and have black hats on their heads so high!

(*Gesturing, impassioned*) *Then* you will have to go in amongst all those gentlemen, and when your turn comes and you cannot read, nor even spell the words without mistakes, then you will see how the gentlemen will laugh and make fun of you! (*Hands on her hips*) See how you like that!

HANS BRINKER or the SILVER SKATES

Set in Holland in the 1840s, the story of Hans Brinker or The
Silver Skates *by Mary Mapes Dodge records how the Brinker
children, Hans and Gretel, long for a pair of real ice skates.
However, there is no money for such luxuries due to their
father's accident ten years earlier, an accident that has
seriously affected his mind and memory. In order to
supplement the family income, Hans and Gretel do whatever
they can, and their mother ekes out a meager living from
raising vegetables, spinning and knitting. She even works on a
barge, where she is occasionally harnessed with other women to
a towing rope. But when Hans grows strong and large, he
insists upon doing all such drudgery in her place. Dame
Brinker does her best to control her husband, who is physically
strong but possesses the mind of a child. But she still loves him
and tenderly cares for him because he was a good and steady
husband.*

*In this scene, Gretel has been told to wait outside while
doctors examine her father.*

GRETEL

How loud the moans are behind the darkened window;
what if those strange men are really killing my father!
(*Leaping to her feet in horror*) Ah! no, (*Sobbing*) Mother is
there, and Hans. They will care for him. But how pale
they were. And even Hans was crying!

Why did that cross old doctor keep *him* and send me
away? I could have clung to mother and kissed her. That
always makes her stroke my hair and speak gently, even

after she has scolded me. How quiet it is now! Oh, if father should die, and Hans, and Mother, what *would* I do? Why didn't Hans tell me? It is a shame! It is my father as well as his. I am no baby. I once took a sharp knife from father's hand. I even drew him away from Mother on that awful night when Hans, big as he is, could not help her. Why, then, should I be treated like one who can do nothing? Oh, how very still it is—how bitter, bitter cold!

God has taken care of father so long, He would do it still if those men would only leave! (*Listening*) Ah, now those men are on the roof; they are clambering to the top! Oh, no—it's Mother and Hans—or the storks—it is so dark, who can tell?

(*Growing sleepy*) How sweetly the birds are singing. They must be winter birds, for the air is thick with icicles—not one bird—but twenty! Oh! Hear them, Mother—wake me for the race, Mother—I am so tired with crying and crying . . . (*She dozes off*)

A LITTLE PRINCESS

Sara in Frances Hodgson Burnett's A Little Princess *is a very serious child. After her mother dies in India, she becomes her father's companion, and they become very attached. However, her father, Captain Crew, believes she needs schooling, so he brings her to England to Miss Minchin's seminary for young ladies, located in a house that Sara thinks is exactly like Miss Minchin—respectable, well-furnished, ugly, and hard. After Sara's father dies penniless, the cruel Miss Minchin takes away all the lovely things he had bought her and makes Sara work in the kitchen. In this tale of riches to rags, Sara reveals that being a princess is based on character, not money, for Sara is kind and generous in good times and in hard times. In this speech, Sara holds Emily, her doll, and uses the doll to illustrate.*

SARA

I am getting very old, you see, and I shall never live to have another doll given me. This will be my last doll. There is something solemn about it. If I could write poetry, I am sure a poem about "A Last Doll" would be very nice. But I cannot write poetry. I have tried, and it made me laugh. I did not sound like Coleridge or Shakespeare. So I want to tell you about how I found Emily, my companion.

I told Papa that I want her to look as if she isn't a doll, really. I want her to look as if she really listens when I talk to her. The trouble with dolls is that they never really seem to *hear*.

We looked at big ones and little ones—at dolls with black eyes, and dolls with blue—at dolls with brown curls and dolls with golden braids, dolls dressed and dolls undressed until I finally said, "There is Emily! She is actually waiting for us!"

She is a large doll, isn't she? See, she has naturally curling golden-brown hair, which hangs about her like a mantle, don't you think? And her eyes are a deep, clear, gray-blue, with soft, thick eyelashes which are real, not painted, see?

"Of course," I said, holding Emily on my lap and looking into her face, "Of course, this is Emily."

Can't you see how she really listens? Doesn't she have the most understanding face? No matter what I tell her, she listens and understands. I wonder how many people can do that?

WAR and PEACE

Natasha, the beautiful young girl in Tolstoy's War and Peace, *represents all that is lovely and worth fighting for in the old world and nearly loses her love when she is about fifteen years old by mistaking a seduction for a love declaration. In the following speech, Natasha reveals to her cousin, Sonia, her intention to elope with Anatole Kuragin and betray her betrothal to Prince Andrey, whom she has loved since she was eleven years old.*

NATASHA

Oh, if you could only know how happy I am! You don't know what love . . . you don't understand. Listen. (*In reverie*) Three days. It seems to me as though I had loved him for a hundred years. It seems to me that I have never loved anyone before him. (*Patiently*) You can't understand that. (*Increasing excitement*) I have been told of its happening, and no doubt you have heard of it, too, but it's only now that I have felt such love. It's *not* what I have felt before. As soon as I saw him, I felt that he was my sovereign and I was his slave, and that I could not help loving him. (*Defensive*) Yes, his slave! Whatever he bids me, I shall do. You don't understand that. (*Pausing, suddenly afraid*) What am I to do? (*Imploring*) What am I to do? (*Resigned*) I simply have no will. (*Annoyed*) How is it you don't understand that? (*Impassioned*) I love him! I don't care for anyone, I don't love anyone but him! You want to make me miserable, and you want us to be separated . . . if you tell, you are my enemy!

BOYS' MONOLOGUES

THE STEADFAST TIN SOLDIER

The Steadfast Tin Soldier *is a Hans Christian Andersen tale that celebrates differences. The Tin Soldier lives in a box with twenty-five others who are exactly alike; each has a splendid red-and-blue uniform, shoulders his musket, looks directly forward, and stands straight and tall. The Tin Soldier, however, is different. He has only one leg because there hadn't been enough tin to finish him. But in spite of this, he stands just as firmly and erect as the others.*

Spotting a ballerina on the playroom table who is holding one foot in the air, he is immediately attracted because it appears that she, too, has only one leg. But even though he has found his soulmate, he is much too shy to approach her, so the Tin Soldier and the ballerina just stand on the playroom table, staring at each other all day long.

To shorten this piece, you may begin with "I looked around the playroom . . . "

TIN SOLDIER

I came in a box of tin soldiers. Each soldier was exactly like every other soldier. Each one had a splendid red-and-blue uniform. Each one shouldered his musket and looked directly before him. Each one stood straight and tall on the table.

There hadn't been quite enough tin to finish us all, however, so I only had one leg. I stood just as firmly on my one leg as the others stood on their two legs.

I looked around the playroom table at all the other toys. There was a magnificent castle made out of cardboard. In front of the castle was a looking-glass that was supposed to be a lake. Around the lake there were rustling green trees made of paper, and on the lake were white swans made of wax. It was all very handsome, but the handsomest thing by far was a little lady who stood in the doorway of the castle. She was made of paper, too, but she wore a dress of pale blue gauze. The dress had a blue ribbon around the neck, and in the middle of the ribbon was a shining tinsel rose as big as the lady's face.

This lady was a dancer, so she stood up on one toe and kicked her other foot high in the air. There she held it, straight up in the air, and it looked to me as if *she* had only one leg.

"Just like me," I said to myself. "She and I should marry, for she would be a lovely wife."

That is what I said to myself, but I was very shy. I didn't know how to become friends with the lovely lady, so I just stood on the playroom table all day and looked at her.

THE LOST PRINCE

The Lost Prince *by Frances Hodgson Burnett chronicles the adventures of Marco and his father, who are dedicated to saving the kingdom of Samavia from destruction and bringing the Lost Prince home to his people. Marco and his friend, The Rat, a street boy of London, disguise themselves as beggar boys to travel across Europe to Samavia to bring the message that the salvation of Samavia is at hand. They meet in an alley in London. The Rat is a strange little creature with a big forehead, deep eyes that are curiously sharp, and a savage little face marked with lines as if he has been angry all his life. He is also a hunchback whose legs look small and crooked.*

THE RAT

(*The Rat sits, agitated, biting his nails*) Tell you what! This is what happened. It was some of the Maranovich fellows who tried to kill him. They meant to kill his father and make their own man king, and they knew the people wouldn't stand it if young Ivor was alive. They just stabbed him in the back, the fiends! I dare say they heard the old shepherd coming, and left him for dead and ran.

(*Feverish, still biting his nails*) When he got well, he couldn't go back. He was only a boy. The other fellow had been crowned, and his followers felt strong because they'd just conquered the country. He could have done nothing without an army, and he was too young to raise one. Perhaps he thought he'd wait till he was old enough to know what to do. I dare say he went away and had to work for his living as if he'd never been a prince at all.

(*Pacing*) Then perhaps sometime he had a son, and told him who he was and how he had been driven from his home. (*Quickening his pace, vengeful*) I'd have told him. I'd have told him that if I couldn't get back the throne, he must do so when he grew to be a man. And I'd have made him swear, when he got it back, to take it out on them, or their children, or their children's children; that's what I'd have done.

The Rat tells a harrowing tale of abuse and its results for a young hunchbacked boy.

THE RAT
Second Speech

I call myself "The Rat." Look at me! Crawling around on the ground like this! Look at me! (*The Rat contorts his face and body and begins darting around the stage, uttering sharp squeaks; he then stands and faces the audience*) Wasn't I like a rat? I feel like one. Everyone's my enemy. I am vermin. I can't fight or defend myself unless I bite. (*Sarcastically*) I can bite, though! (*Baring his teeth menacingly*) I bite my father when he gets drunk and beats me. I've bitten him till he's learned to remember. (*Laughing shrilly*) He hasn't tried it for three months— even when he *was* drunk—and he's *always* drunk. (*Laughing raucously*) He's a gentleman. I'm a *gentleman's* son. He was a master at a big school until he was kicked out—that was when I was four, and mother died. I'm thirteen now.

HUCKLEBERRY FINN

In Mark Twain's Huckleberry Finn, Huck, the fourteen-year-old son of the town drunk, has fascinated readers of all ages since its appearance in 1884. Huck's naiveté and innocence often make his narration unintentionally funny, and his genuine good heart endures through all social changes. In his adventures down the Mississippi on a raft with the runaway slave, Jim, Huck meets all kinds of people. In this episode, he has gone ashore and run into the feuding Grangerfords and Shepherdsons.

HUCKLEBERRY FINN

Emmeline Grangerford kept a scrapbook when she was alive, and used to paste obituaries and accidents and cases of patient suffering in it out of the *Presbyterian Observer*, and write poetry after them out of her own head. It was very good poetry.

Buck said she could rattle off poetry like nothing. She didn't ever have to stop to think. He said she would slap down a line, and if she couldn't find anything to rhyme with it, would just scratch it out and slap down another one and go ahead.

She warn't particular; she could write about anything you choose to give her to write about, just so it was sadful. Every time a man died, or a woman died, or a child died, she would be on hand with her "tribute" before he was cold. She called them tributes. The neighbors said it was the doctor first, then Emmeline, then the undertaker—the undertaker never got in ahead of Emmeline but once. She warn't the same after that. She never complained, but she kinder pined away and did not live long. (*Pensive*) Poor thing. Many's the time I made myself go up to the little room that used to be hers and get out her poor old scrapbook and read in it when her pictures had been aggravating me and I had soured on her a little. She made poetry about all the dead people when she was alive, and it didn't seem right that there warn't nobody to make some about her, now she was gone; so I tried to sweat out a verse or two myself—but I couldn't seem to make it go, somehow.

Huck and Jim have helped the duke and the king escape a mob on shore, but once on the raft, the two men begin quarreling over who is more important. When they finally compromise, Huck and Jim are greatly relieved.

HUCKLEBERRY FINN
Second Speech

The duke and the king done made up, and Jim and me was pretty glad to see it. It took away all the uncomfortableness and we felt mighty good over it, because it woulda been a miserable business to have any unfriendliness on the raft, for what you want, above all things, on a raft, is for everybody to be satisfied, and feel right and kind towards the others.

It didn't take me long to make up my mind that these liars warn't no kings nor dukes at all, but just low-down humbugs and frauds. But I never said nothin'; never let on; kept it to myself; it's the best way; then you don't have no quarrels and don't get into no trouble. If they wanted us to call them kings and dukes, I hadn't no objections, 'long as it would keep peace in the family; and it warn't no use to tell Jim, so I didn't tell him. If I never learnt nothing else outta pap, I learnt that the best way to get along with his kind of people is to let them have their own way.

STREET LIFE in NEW YORK

Horatio Alger wrote boys' tales from the 1860s to the 1890s to teach young boys the value of honesty, hard work, and cheerfulness in the face of adversity. These rags-to-riches stories illustrate the popular American dream that good fortune awaits everyone who is willing to work for it. Dick, *the hero of* Ragged Dick, *is a diamond in the rough. He is a slum boy who is streetwise and cocky but has an innate virtue.*

DICK

I don't know enough to hurt me. All I know about readin' you could put in a nutshell, and there'd be room left for a small family. I know all my letters, but not intimately. I can call 'em all by name.

I went two days to school, but it didn't agree with my constitution. I found lickin's didn't agree with me. I got punished awful, just for indulgin' a little harmless amusement. You see, the boy that was sittin' next to me fell asleep, which I consider improper in school-time; so I thought I'd help the teacher a little by wakin' him up. So I took a pin and stuck into him; but I guess it went a little too far, for he screeched awful. The teacher found out what it was that made him holler, and whipped me with a ruler till I was black and blue. I thought 'twas about time to take a vacation—so that's the last time I went to school.

Dick's life on the streets has taught him self-reliance. In the following passage, however, we see that he is honest, as Alger heroes must be.

DICK
Second Speech

I ain't knocked 'round the city streets all my life for nothin'. I changed my business accordin' as I had to. Sometimes I was a newsboy, and diffused intelligence among the masses, as I heard somebody say once in a big speech he made in the park. But I give it up after a while.

They didn't always put enough news in their papers, and people wouldn't buy 'em as fast as I wanted 'em to. So one mornin' I was stuck with a lot of *Heralds*, and I thought I'd make a sensation. So I called out, "*Great news! Queen Victoria Assassinated!*" All my *Heralds* went off like hotcakes, and I went off, too, but one of the gentlemen who got sold remembered me, and said he'd have me took up, and that's what made me change my business. (*Confidentially*) I was sort of ashamed at the time, 'specially about one poor old gentleman—a Englishman he was. He couldn't help cryin' to think the Queen was dead, and his hands shook when he handed me the money for the paper.

I've knowed what it was to be hungry and cold, with nothin' to eat or to warm me; but there's one thing I never could do—(*Holding his head high*) I never stole. It's mean, and I wouldn't do it.

THE LITTLE BOY and the DIKE

The story of the little boy who holds back the water to save all the townspeople is a popular legend from Holland that celebrates the quiet heroism of an ordinary boy. The nameless Dutch boy passes one of the many dikes (dams to hold back the water that surrounds Holland) around the village he lives in and hears a leak. Without concern for his own safety, he rushes over and plugs the leak with his finger. He remains in this position all night until a villager comes by the next morning. You might start with "Without even stopping to think . . . " and go through the next paragraph up to " . . . my nice soft bed" and cut from there to "No, I had to stay there myself . . . " (toward the end of paragraph five) to the end.

BOY

I heard a soft gurgling noise, as though a little stream of water were flowing through a hole. I stopped and bent down, trying to see what made the noise, even though I felt sure there could be no hole in the large, strong dike. But as I looked, I saw a tiny leak and water flowing through it.

Without even stopping to think, I slipped down to the bottom of the dike and put my finger in the little hole to keep the water from coming through. Then I looked around for someone to help me, someone to bring word of the leak to the men in the village; but the road was deserted, and no one was in sight. I shouted loudly, hoping that someone in a nearby field would hear my calls and come to help me. But only my own echo answered.

It was lonely there. I was hungry and tired. My fingers grew stiff as, one after the other, they kept the hole in the dike plugged up. I thought of mother and father and sister waiting for me in the little cottage on the edge of the tulip field. I thought of the supper waiting for me, and of my nice soft bed.

But I also thought of what would happen if I deserted my post, if I let the water leak through the hole in the dike. I knew that the water would wash the earth and rock away, making the hole larger and larger, until at last a strong stream of water would flow through and flood the fields and the houses and the windmills.

I looked for something to plug up the leak so that I could go to the village for help. I put a stone in the hole and then a stick, but each in turn was washed out by the force of the water. No, I had to stay there myself and use all my strength if the water were to be kept out. All night long, I stayed at my post. My fingers grew cold and numb and my whole body longed to sleep, but I knew that I had to be strong and patient; I could not give up.

Early in the morning, I heard the welcome sound that told me someone was coming along the road—that help was near at last.

PETER PAN

Peter Pan is the boy who refuses to grow up. James Barry's hero lives in Never-Never Land with a fairy named Tinkerbell for a companion. He convinces Wendy and her brothers to join the Lost Boys. While in Never-Never Land, the children fight the evil Captain Hook. Here, Peter tells how he came to be a Lost Boy:

PETER

I ran away the day I was born.

It was because I heard father and mother talking about what I was to be when I became a man. (*Dismayed*) I don't want *ever* to be a man! I want *always* to be a little boy and have *fun*. (*Matter-of-factly*) So I ran away to Kensington Gardens and lived a long time among the fairies.

(*Earnest*) You see, when the first baby laughed for the first time, its laugh broke into a thousand pieces, and they all went skipping about, and that was the beginning of fairies; (*Affably*) and now, there is one fairy for every girl and boy.

(*Disheartened*) But you see, children know such a lot now, they soon don't believe in fairies, and every time a child says, "I don't believe in fairies," there is a fairy somewhere that falls down dead.

POLLYANNA

Pollyanna, the persistently optimistic orphan, tries to get her Aunt Polly to adopt Jimmy like she has gotten Aunt Polly to adopt a kitten and puppy, but Jimmy is not an animal; he's a real boy with real feelings. He's annoyed with Pollyanna's insistence on knowing his story. He speaks with anger and hurt pride at first, but despairs at the end. He is poor and ragged but proud.

JIMMY

All right, then—here goes! I'm Jimmy Bean, and I'm ten years old goin' on eleven. I come last year ter live at the Orphan's Home. But they've got so many kids there ain't much room for me, an' I wa'n't never wanted, anyhow, I don't believe. So I've quit. I'm goin' ter live somewheres else—but I hain't found the place yet. I'd *like* a home—jest a common one, ye know, with a mother in it, instead of a matron. If ye has a home, ye has folks; an' I hain't had folks since—Dad died. So I'm a-huntin' now. I've tried four houses, but—they didn't want me—though I said I spected ter work, 'course.

(*He sighs, considering*) Maybe I better go back, fer tonight—ter the Home. You see, I hain't no other place to stay, and—I didn't leave till this mornin'. I slipped out. I didn't tell 'em I wasn't comin' back, else they'd pretend I couldn't come; though I'm thinkin' they won't do no worryin' when I don't show up sometime. (*Dejected*) They ain't like folks, ye know. (*Incredulous*) They don't *care*!

TOM SAWYER

This delightful scene from Mark Twain's Tom Sawyer *is well-known.*

As punishment, his Aunt Polly has ordered Tom to whitewash a fence on Saturday, his day of freedom and fun. But Tom is a clever trickster who makes work look like so much fun that other boys beg him to be allowed to do it.

As you deliver the speech, act out the situation. A straw hat worn to the back of the head, overalls, a paint brush, and an apple will bring Tom to life.

TOM SAWYER

Here comes Ben! (*He begins to whitewash attentively. After a bit he stands back to view the effect studiously, as if he's a painter, ignoring the onlooker*)
What's that you say, Ben? Oh, you go along and play with your truck or whatever. I'm kinda busy. Oh, you think this is work? Well . . . whatever. (*He keeps brushing back and forth, stepping back to criticize the effect*)
I'm sorry! What did you say? You wanna paint some? Oh, I don't think Aunt Polly'd like me to let you paint. She's awful particular about this fence. (*Faking reluctance*) I'd love to let ya, but I don't know—Aunt Polly did trust me.
What? You'll give me your apple. Naw . . .
Well-l-l, that apple sure looks good. Maybe . . . Oh! Okay, just for a little while! (*He sits down with Ben's apple and begins munching. He turns to the audience*)

I gave up the brush with reluctance in my face, but alacrity in my heart. And while Ben worked and sweated in the sun, I sat on a barrel in the shade close by, dangled my legs, munched his apple, and planned the slaughter of more innocents.

There was no lack of material; boys happened along every little while; they came to jeer, but remained to whitewash. When Ben got tired out, I traded the next chance to Billy Fisher for a kite, in good repair; and when *he* played out, Johnny Miller bought in for a dead rat and a string to swing it with—and so on and so on, hour after hour. By the middle of the afternoon I was rolling in wealth. If I hadn't run out of whitewash, I would've bankrupted every boy in the village.

Tom is a well-meaning boy, but he likes adventure so much that he often forgets the suffering he causes. After running away, he and his friend, Joe Harper, pretend to be dead and even attend their own funeral.

Back safely at home, Tom is recalling a "dream" to his aunt that is actually an account of a secret visit he paid her during the time he was thought to be dead.

TOM SAWYER
Second Speech

(*Ill at ease*) Now, Auntie, you know I do care for you . . . I dreamed about you, anyway. (*Hopeful*) That's something, ain't it?

(*With a great show of remembering*) Wednesday night I dreamt that you was sitting over there by the bed, and Sid was sitting by the woodbox, and Mary next to him. (*Slowly, with effort*) And I dreamt that Joe Harper's mother was here—but it's so dim now. . . (*Haltingly*) Somehow it seems to me that the wind—the wind blowed the . . . the . . . (*Pausing for emphasis.*) I've got it! I've got it now! It blowed out the candle! And it seems to me that she said, "Why, I believe that the door . . ." (*Faltering*) Just let me study a moment—just a moment. Oh, yes, she said she believed the door was open.

And then . . . and then . . . well, I won't be certain, but it seems as if she made Sid go and . . . and . . . she made him . . . (*With tremendous relief*) oh! She made him shut it! Oh, it's all getting just as bright as day now. Next she said I warn't *bad*, only mischeevous and harum-scarum, and not any more responsible than . . . than . . . I think it was a colt, or something. (*Sorrowful*) And then you began to cry. Then Mrs. Harper began to cry, and said Joe was just the same and she wished she hadn't whipped him for taking cream when she'd throwed it out her own self. And then there was talk of dragging the river for us, and 'bout having the funeral Sunday, and you and ole Miss Harper hugged and cried, and she went. (*Genuinely moved*) Then I thought you prayed for me . . . and I could hear every word you said. And you went to bed, and I was so sorry that I took and wrote on a piece of sycamore bark, "We ain't dead . . . we are only off being pirates," and put it on the table by the candle; and then you looked so good, laying there asleep, that I thought I went and leaned over and kissed you on the cheek.

THE WIND in the WILLOWS

Kenneth Graham's nighttime tales and summer letters to his son became The Wind in the Willows. *This delightful story of Rat, Mole, Badger, and Toad has continued to intrigue generations of children.*

Here, in Rat's speech, he is hypnotized by his own rhapsody about river life.

RAT

Believe me, there is nothing—absolutely nothing—half so much worth doing as simply messing about in boats. Simply messing—(*Dreamily*) messing—about—in—boats; about in boats—(*Regaining his composure*) in or out of 'em, it doesn't matter. *Nothing* seems really to matter, that's the charm of it. Whether you get away, or whether you don't; whether you arrive at your destination or whether you reach somewhere else, or whether you never get anywhere at all, you're always busy, and you never do anything in particular; and when you've done it, there's always something else to do, and you can do it if you like, but you'd much better not.

(*Inspired*) Look here! If you've really nothing else on hand this morning, supposing we drop down the river together, and have a long day of it?

On their adventure, Rat and Mole have passed by Mole's old home, but Rat didn't realize it. Mole has tried, but is unable to contain his homesickness and pain.

MOLE

(*Sobbing brokenly*) I know it's a . . . shabby, dingy little place, not like . . . your cozy quarters . . . or Toad's beautiful hall . . . or Badger's great house . . . but it was my own little home . . . and I was fond of it . . . and I went away and forgot all about it—and then I smelt it suddenly . . . on the road, and I called and you wouldn't listen, Rat . . . and everything came back to me with a rush . . . and I *wanted* it! . . . O dear! O dear! . . . and when you *wouldn't* turn back, Ratty . . . and I had to leave it, though I was smelling it all the time . . . I thought my heart would break. . . . We might have just gone and had one look at it, Ratty . . . only one look . . . it was close by . . . but you wouldn't turn back, Ratty, you wouldn't turn back! O dear, O dear!

(*Shaking his head*) I never meant to let you know I was feeling that way about it . . . it was all an accident and a mistake! (*Alarmed, searching, at last spying Ratty offstage*) Wherever are you (hic) going to (hic), Ratty? (*Getting up to run after him*) O, come back, Ratty do!

Toad is an irrepressible charmer who never seems to learn any lesson. He has almost escaped capture, but in his arrogance, he has stopped to sing his triumph, allowing his captors to overtake him.

TOAD

(*Frenzied throughout*) O horror! O misery! O despair! O my! What an ass I am! What a conceited and heedless ass! Swaggering again! Shouting and singing songs again! Sitting still and gassing again! O my! O my! O my! If I *ever* steal a motor-car again! If I ever sing another conceited song!

(*Pacing*) This is the end of everything. At least it is the end of the career of *Toad*, which is the same thing; the popular and handsome Toad, the rich and hospitable Toad, the Toad so free and careless and debonair! How can I hope to be ever set at large again who have been imprisoned so *justly* for stealing so handsome a motor-car with such an audacious manner, and for such lurid and imaginative cheek, bestowed upon such a number of fat, red-faced policemen!

(*Crumpling into a seat, resigned*) Stupid animal that I was, now I must languish in this dungeon till people, who were proud to say they knew me, have forgotten the very *name* of Toad! O wise old Badger! O clever, intelligent Rat and sensible Mole! What sound judgments, what a knowledge of men and matters you possess! O unhappy and forsaken Toad!

LITTLE MEN

Louisa May Alcott's Little Women *was so popular that she wrote a sequel,* Little Men, *which follows the story of Jo, the writer, and her husband, Professor Bhaer, at Plumfield, their school for boys. Tom, one of the students at Plumfield, whose father is rich, speaks here; he's proud to be able to do something for Dan, a poor boy who had been unfairly blamed for a theft.*

TOM

(*Importantly*) We fellows were talking over the late interesting case of circumstantial evidence, and I proposed giving Dan something to make up for our suspecting him, to show our respect, and so on, you know—something handsome and useful, that he could keep always, and be proud of.

We have decided on a microscope. (*Eagerly*) A real swell one, that we see what-do-you-call-'ems in water with, and stars, and ant eggs, and all sorts of games, you know. Won't it be a good present?

(*Apologetic*) Of course, it will cost a lot, but we are all going to give something. I headed the paper with my five dollars; for if it is to be done at all, it must be done handsome.

(*Thoughtful*) And, you see, I've been so bothered with my property that I'm tired of it and don't mean to save up any more, but give it away as I go along, and then nobody will envy me, or want to steal it, and I shan't be suspecting folks, and worrying about my old cash.

Mr. Bhaer thought it was a first-rate plan, and said that some of the best men he knew preferred to do good with their money instead of laying it up to be squabbled over when they died.

HEIDI

Peter, the shepherd boy in Heidi, *has been used to having Heidi all to himself, so he grows more and more jealous of Heidi's friend from the city, Klara, who takes all of Heidi's time and attention. Klara is crippled and uses a wheelchair that Peter, in a jealous rage, pushes off a mountain.*

Peter is very angry and acts out his account as he tells it. You can shorten the speech by cutting from " . . . instantly disappeared . . . " to "Far below me . . . " and leaving out the last paragraph.

PETER

My eyes fell on the chair, which was standing so proudly on its rollers, and seemed to stare at me like an enemy; an enemy that had already done me so much harm, and to-day would do still more.

I looked about. Everything was quiet, nobody in sight. Like a wild creature I threw myself upon the chair, seized hold of it, and gave it a mighty shove toward the steepest part of the decline. Away flew the chair, and instantly disappeared.

I rushed up the Alm, not stopping until I reached a big blackberry bush, behind which I concealed myself. I had no desire for my uncle to catch sight of me; I was anxious to see what would become of the chair, nevertheless, and this bush was placed most conveniently on the edge of a spur. What a wonderful thing met my view! Far below me, my enemy was plunging down, as if driven by an ever-increasing power. It turned over and over, made a big leap, then threw itself down again on the earth and rushed to its ruin. Bits of it flew in every direction: feet, arms, cushions, everything was thrown into the air.

I felt such an unbounded joy at the sight that I jumped up with both feet together. I laughed aloud; I stamped for joy; I leaped about in a circle; I ran to the same place again and looked down, broke into laughter again, and again leaped about. I was beside myself with delight at the overthrow of my enemy. Now surely the stranger would be obliged to go away, because she would have no means of moving about. Now everything could go back to the old order.

Davy is about six years old, one of twins, and is considered a bit of a handful. He does like (and sometimes minds) Anne in Anne of Avonlea. *He should be very self-important in this speech.*

DAVY

Well, it was partly accident that Paul fell in the brook; he stuck his head in on purpose, but the rest of him fell in accidentally. We was all down at the brook and Prillie Rogerson got mad at Paul about something—she's awful mean and horrid anyway, even if she is pretty—and said that his grandmother put his hair up in curl rags every night. Paul wouldn't have minded what she said, I guess, but Gracie Andrews laughed, and Paul got awful red, 'cause Gracie's his girl, you know. He's *clean gone* on her—brings her flowers and carries her books as far as the shore road. He got as red as a beet and said his grandmother didn't do any such thing and his hair was born curly. And then he laid down on the bank and stuck his head right into the spring to show them. (*Hastening to explain*) Oh, it wasn't the spring we drink out of, it was the little one lower down. But the bank's awful slippy, and Paul went right in.

I tell you, he made a splendid splash! But he looked so funny when he crawled out, all wet and muddy . . . the girls laughed more'n ever, but Gracie didn't laugh. She looked sorry. Gracie's a nice girl, but she's got a snub nose. When I get big enough to have a girl, I won't have one with a snub nose. And I'll wash my face before I go courting. And I'll wash behind my ears, too, without being told. (*Proudly*) I remembered this morning. I don't forget half as often as I did—it's just there's so many corners about a fellow, it's hard to remember them all.

AN IROQUOIS MYTH

The young boy in this creation myth recounts his birth and his feats at the beginning of time. He's strong and eloquent and speaks rhythmically. He may play a drum, or it can play softly offstage. You may want to stop after paragraph two, " . . . from whom was to spring all life."

YOUNG BOY

I am Hah-gweh-di-yu. At my birth, my Sky Mother, Ata-en-sic, died, and the island was still dim in the dawn of its new life when, grieving at my mother's death, I shaped the sky with the palm of my hand, and creating the Sun from her face, lifted it there, saying, "You shall rule here where your face will shine forever." But Hah-gweh-da-et-gah set Darkness in the west sky, to drive the Sun down behind it.

I then drew forth from the breast of my mother the Moon and the Stars, and led them to the Sun as my sisters, who would guard the night sky. I gave to the Earth her body, its Great Mother, from whom was to spring all life.

All over the land I planted towering mountains, and in the valleys set high hills to protect the straight rivers as they ran to sea. But Hah-gweh-da-et-gah wrathfully sundered the mountains, hurling them far apart, and drove the high hills into the wavering valleys, bending the rivers as he hunted them down.

I set forests on the high hills, and on the low plains fruit-bearing trees and vines to wing their seeds to the scattering winds. But Hah-gweh-da-et-gah gnarled the forests besetting the Earth, and led monsters to dwell in the sea, and herded hurricanes in the sky, which frowned with mad tempests that chased the Sun and the Stars.

GREAT EXPECTATIONS

Pip in Charles Dickens' Great Expectations is an orphan being raised by his sister and her husband. He goes often to the cemetery to visit his parents' graves. This time, however, a convict finds him and threatens to kill him and his sister and her husband, Joe, if Pip doesn't agree to bring him a file and some food.

PIP

(*Bellowing gruffly*) "Keep still, you little devil, or I'll cut your throat!"

(*Recounting, wide-eyed*) A fearful man, all in coarse gray, with a great iron on his leg started up from among the graves at the side of the church porch; a man with no hat, and broken shoes, and an old rag tied around his head. A man who had been soaked in water, and smothered in mud, and lamed by stones, and cut by flints, and stung by nettles, and torn by briars; who limped, and shivered, and glared, and growled; and whose teeth chattered in his head as he seized me by the chin.

"Please sir! Don't cut my throat! Pip! Pip's my name, please, sir!"

The man looked at me for a moment, turned me upside down, and emptied my pockets. There was nothing in them but a piece of bread. He set me far up on a high tombstone, and I watched, trembling, as he ate the bread.

The question, he said, was whether or not I was to live. He came closer to my tombstone, took me by both arms, and tilted me back as far as he could hold me; his eyes looked down most powerfully into mine, and mine looked most helplessly up into his.

"Do you know what a file is and what wittles* is?" he demanded.

"Yes, sir!" I was dreadfully frightened, and so giddy that I clung to him with both hands and said, "If you would kindly please to let me keep upright, sir, perhaps I shouldn't be so sick, and perhaps I could attend more." (*Queasy*) He gave me the most tremendous dip and roll, then held me by the arms upright above the stone.

"Swear to God that you'll be back here in the morning with that file and wittles!"

"I swear," I whispered.

"What?" he roared.

"I swear," I said more forcefully.

"You better be," he said, moving off into the marsh, "or I'll find you and kill you and all your family."

I turned and ran toward home, seeing his raging eyes all the way.

---

* food

THE VELVETEEN RABBIT

The rabbit in Margery Bianco's The Velveteen Rabbit *has stayed with his young boy during all his sickness, staying under the covers to offer the boy what comfort he could.*

RABBIT

I remember the day the boy became ill. His face grew flushed, and he talked in his sleep, and his body was so hot that it burned me when he held me close. Strange people came and went in the nursery, and a lamp burned all night. I lay there, hidden from sight under the bedclothes, and never stirred, for I was afraid that if they found me, someone might take me away—and I knew the boy needed me. It was a long, weary time, for the boy was too ill to play, and I found it rather dull with nothing to do all day long; but I snuggled down patiently, and looked forward to the time the boy would be well again, and we would go out in the garden and play splendid games in the raspberry thicket like we used to. While the boy lay half asleep, I crept up close to the pillow and whispered this in his ear; and presently, the fever turned, and the boy got better. One morning they carried the boy out on to the balcony, leaving me tangled up among the bedclothes. With just my head peeking out, I listened as they spoke of plans to take the boy to the seaside. The boy had often talked of the seaside, and I wanted very much to see the big waves coming in, and the tiny crabs, and the sand castles. Hurrah! We were going to the seashore!

THE HAPPY PRINCE

In Oscar Wilde's fairy tale The Happy Prince *the Prince is a very rich statue. He is gilded all over with thin leaves of fine gold. For eyes he has two bright sapphires. A large red ruby glows on his sword-hilt. This statue provides a model for many. For children, it is a symbol for not crying for anything; for disappointed people ,it is a symbol of joy; and for those striving, it is a symbol of perfection. The statue, however, unlike The Happy Prince, is not walled off from people; he can see poverty and misery around him. A swallow, who has not gone to warmer climates, becomes his helper, taking the gold leaf from the statue and bringing it to the poor until the bird freezes to death. At the end, though, the statue's lead heart and the swallow's frozen body go to the garden of heaven, where they will live happily ever after for their human kindness.*

THE PRINCE

I am the Happy Prince.

When I was alive and had a human heart, I did not know what tears were; I lived in the palace of Sans-Souci, where sorrow is not allowed to enter. In the daytime I played with my companions in the garden, and in the evening I led the dance in the Great Hall. Round the garden ran a very lofty wall, but I never cared to ask what lay beyond it, everything about me was so wonderful. My courtiers called me The Happy Prince, and happy indeed I was, if pleasure be happiness. So I lived, and so I died. And now that I am dead, they have set me up here so high that I can see all the ugliness and all the misery of my city, and though my heart is made of lead, yet I cannot choose but weep.

Far away, in a little street, there is a poor house. One of the windows is open, and through it I can see a woman at a table. Her face is thin and worn; she is embroidering flowers on a satin gown for one of the Queen's maids. In a bed in the corner of the room, her little boy is lying ill. He has a fever, and is asking for oranges; his mother has nothing to give him but river water, so he is crying. Swallow, will you not bring her the ruby out of my sword-hilt? My feet are fastened to this pedestal, and I cannot move.

THE UGLY DUCKLING

The Ugly Duckling by Hans Christian Andersen is the story of a swan who is placed with ducklings as a chick, so he grows up thinking he is an ugly duckling. When he goes on the water, however, as a grown-up swan, he's beautiful and graceful.

SWAN

I am so ugly, I am bitten and pushed and made fun of by both the ducks *and* the chickens. Even my brothers and sisters make fun of me. I thought that someday they would grow accustomed to my looks—but they never do. I hoped that some would point out what an excellent disposition I have, or notice how well I swim; but they never do. Each day I grow more unhappy. All I want is to get away from the farmyard; I want to go where there are no animals at all—where no one can call me ugly.

I'm going to run away. (*Half running and half flying*) There! I'm over the fence! I know where this is—it's the great marsh where the wild ducks live. I'll lie here among the reeds and drink a little water from the marsh.

What's that?! It sounds like dogs! Oh! Look at him— he's horrible! Look at his teeth! Oh no! Here he comes! (*Hides his head under his wing*)

Wait! What happened? (*Amazed*) He just went away!

(*Understanding suddenly.*) I must have been too ugly even for a dog to bite! (*Crys softly*)

ROBINSON CRUSOE

Robinson Crusoe *by Daniel Defoe is the story of a young man who runs away to sea despite not having his father's permission or approval.*

After many harrowing adventures, he's shipwrecked alone on an island inhabited only by cannibals. During this time, he meets Friday, a savage, who becomes his friend and helps him survive on the island.

Here he describes his first voyage.

ROBINSON CRUSOE

Never have any young adventurer's misfortunes, I believe, began sooner or continued longer than mine. The ship no sooner got out of the harbor than the wind began to blow, and the sea to rise in a most frightful manner; and as I had never been at sea before, I was most inexpressibly sick in body and terrified in mind.

I began now seriously to reflect on what I had done, and how justly I was overtaken by the judgment of heaven. I had wickedly left my father's house and abandoned my duty; all the good counsel of my parents, my father's tears, and my mother's entreaties came now fresh into my mind, and reproached me with the contempt of advice.

All the while the storm increased and the sea, which I had never been upon before, went very high. I expected every wave to swallow us up, and every time the ship fell down, I feared that we should rise no more.

In this agony of mind I made my vows and resolutions, that if it would please God to spare my life this one voyage, if I ever once got my foot upon dry land again, I would go directly home to my father—and never set it back upon a ship.

LORNA DOONE

John Ridd, the hero of Lorna Doone, *dreams sometimes of escape from all the battling in the valleys of Exmoor, where he lives in the time of James II and the Monmouth Rebellion.*

JOHN RIDD

Oftentimes, I am so vexed by things I cannot meddle with, yet cannot keep away from me, that I am at the point of flying from this dreadful valley—risking all that can betide me, in the unknown outer world. If it were not for my grandfather, I would have done so long ago; but I cannot bear that he should die, with no gentle hand to comfort him; and I fear to think of the conflict—that must ensue for the government—if there be a disputed succession.

Lately, indeed, I had the offer of escape, and kinsman's aid, and high place in the bright world; and yet I was not tempted much—or, at least, dared not to trust it. Still, it has ended very sadly—so dreadfully that I even shrink from telling you about it; for it is the one terror that has changed my life, in a moment, from childhood and thoughts of play, to sense of death and darkness and a heavy weight of earth.

FILMOGRAPHY
Titles available on video and/or laser disc

Alice in Wonderland. U.S., Walt Disney, 1951, 75 minutes, Technicolor,
video and laser disc.

Little Women. U.S., MGM, 1949, 122 minutes, Technicolor,
video and laser disc.

*Little Women.*U.S., Columbia/Tristar (Denise DiNovi), 1994, 118
minutes, color, video and laser disc.

Sense and Sensibility. GB, Columbia Pictures (Mirage Productions),
1995, 136 minutes, color, video and laser disc.

Jane Eyre. U.S., TFC (William Goetz), 1943, 96 minutes, black and
white, video.

Heidi U.S., TCF (Raymond Griffith), 1937, 88 minutes, black and
white, video.

War and Peace. U.S./Italy, Carol Ponti/Dino de Laurentis, 1956, 208
minutes, Technicolor, laser disc.

War and Peace. USSR, Mosfilm, 1967, 507 minutes, Scope 70mm,
video.

The Adventures of Tom Sawyer. U.S., David O. Selznick (William H.
Wright), 1938, 91 minutes, Technicolor, laser disc.

Great Expectations. GB, Rank/Cineguild (Anthony Havellock-Allan),
1946, 118 minutes, black and white, video and laser disc.

ORDER DIRECT

MONOLOGUES THEY HAVEN'T HEARD, Karshner. Modern speeches written in the language of today. $8.95.

MORE MONOLOGUES THEY HAVEN'T HEARD, Karshner. More exciting living-language speeches. $8.95.

SCENES THEY HAVEN'T SEEN, Karshner. Modern scenes for men and women. $7.95.

FOR WOMEN: MONOLOGUES THEY HAVEN'T HEARD, Pomerance. Contemporary speeches for actresses. $8.95

MONOLOGUES FOR KIDS, Roddy. 28 wonderful speeches for boys and girls. $8.95.

MORE MONOLOGUES for KIDS, Roddy. More great speeches for boys and girls. $8.95.

SCENES for KIDS, Roddy. 30 scenes for girls and boys. $8.95.

MONOLOGUES for TEENAGERS, Karshner. Contemporary teen speeches. $8.95.

SCENES for TEENAGERS, Karshner. Scenes for today's teen boys and girls. $7.95.

HIGH-SCHOOL MONOLOGUES THEY HAVEN'T HEARD, Karshner. Contemporary speeches for high-schoolers, $8.95.

MONOLOGUES from the CLASSICS, ed. Karshner. $7.95.

SHAKESPEARE'S MONOLOGUES THEY HAVEN'T HEARD, ed. Dotterer. Lesser-known speeches from The Bard. $7.95.

MONOLOGUES from CHEKHOV, trans. Cartwright. $8.95.

MONOLOGUES from GEORGE BERNARD SHAW, ed. Michaels. $7.95.

MONOLOGUES from OSCAR WILDE, ed. Michaels. The best of Wilde's urbane, dramatic writing from his greatest plays. For men and women. $7.95.

WOMAN, Pomerance. Monologues for actresses. $8.95.

MODERN SCENES for WOMEN, Pomerance. Scenes for today's actresses. $7.95.

MONOLOGUES from MOLIÈRE, trans. Dotterer. A definitive collection of speeches from the French Master. The first translation into English prose. $9.95.

SHAKESPEARE'S MONOLOGUES for WOMEN, ed. Dotterer. $8.95.

DIALECT MONOLOGUES, Karshner/Stern. 13 essential dialects applied to contemporary monologues. Book and cassette tape. $19.95.

YOU SAID a MOUTHFUL, Karshner. Tongue twisters galore. Great exercises for actors, singers, public speakers. Fun for everyone. $7.95.

TEENAGE MOUTH, Karshner. Modern monologues for young men and women. $8.95.

SHAKESPEARE'S LADIES, ed. Dtterer. A second book of Shakespeare's monologues for women. With a descriptive text on acting Shakespeare. $7.95.

BETH HENLEY: MONOLOGUES FOR WOMEN, Henley. *Crimes of the Heart*, others. $7.95.

CITY WOMEN, Smith. 20 powerful, urban monologues. Great audition pieces. $7.95.

KIDS' STUFF, Roddy. 30 great audition pieces for children. $7.95.

KNAVES, KNIGHTS, AND KINGS, ed. Dotterer. Shakespeare's speeches for men. $8.95.

DIALECT MONOLOGUES, VOL. II, Karshner/Stern. 14 more important dialects. Farsi, Afrikaans, Asian Indian, etc. Book and cassette tape. $19.95.

RED LICORICE, Tippit. 31 great scene-monologues for preteens. $8.95.

MODERN MONOLOGUES FOR MODERN KIDS, Mauro. $7.95.

A WOMAN SPEAKS: WOMEN FAMOUS, INFAMOUS and UNKNOWN, ed. Cosentino. $9.95.

FITTING IN, Mauro. Modern monoloues for boys and girls. $8.95.

VOICES, ed. Cosentino. Scene-study pieces for women. $9.95.

FOR WOMEN: MORE MONOLOGUES THEY HAVEN'T HEARD, Pomerance. $8.95.

NEIL SIMON MONOLOGUES, ed. Karshner. First authorized collection of speeches from the works of America's foremost playwright. $9.95.

CLASSIC MOUTH, ed. Cosentino. Speeches from the classics for boys and girls. $8.95

Send your check or money order (no cash or COD) plus handling charges of $4.00 for the first book and $1.50 for each additional book. California residents add 8.25 % tax. Send your order to: Dramaline Publications, 36-851 Palm View Road, Rancho Mirage, California 92270.